COME BACK to me my BOOMERANG

Thanks to Juliet for her constructive thoughts
and creative queries, and to Henrietta and Megan
for seeing things through.

ORCHARD BOOKS
96 Leonard Street, London EC2A 4XD
Orchard Books Australia
Unit 31/56 O'Riordan Street, Alexandria, NSW 2015
First published in Great Britain in 2001
ISBN 1 84121 748 4
Text © John Agard 2001
Illustrations © Lydia Monks 2001
The rights of John Agard to be identified as the author and
Lydia Monks to be identified as the illustrator of this work
have been asserted by them in accordance with the
Copyright, Designs and Patents Act, 1988.
A CIP catalogue record for this book is available from the British Library
10 9 8 7 6 5 4 3 2 1
Printed in Great Britain

COME BACK to me my BOOMERANG

poems by JOHN AGARD

pictures by LYDIA MONKS

ORCHARD BOOKS

To the shapes that shape us
JA

To Kieran
LM

Contents

Come Back to me, my Boomerang

Come back to me, my boomerang
Come back to me as fast as you can.

I threw you from Down Under
All the way to Over Yonder
somewhere past Beyond.

I can't believe you're gone
And the wind will not answer
And the horizon isn't much help.

Come back to me, my boomerang
Come back to me as fast as you can.

I have no time to wait forever
and no more wood to make another.

If Circles Were Square

If circles
were square

would square bubbles
be called squbbles?

And when I blow
would they float
up to the air
in neat rows?

One thing I know
and that's for sure.
If circles
were square

my ball
no longer round
wouldn't roll anymore

and instead of rounders
I'd be playing
squounders.

And Then There Were Ten

1   stands like a soldier upright

2   takes a dip from left to right

3   likes to balance on its hip

4   nudges with an elbow tip

5   does a back-flip on its tummy

6 rolls on its head for all to see

7 leans on a stick yet keeps its back straight

8 writes its name in ice with a skate

9 dances on the tip of its toe

10 says now One has a friend. Zero.

The Top Ten Musical Doughnuts

Now this may sound
like a riddle
says DJ DOUGHNUT
        but
records and CDs
are discs
with a   hole
in the middle
for a musical nibble.

So when DJ DOUGHNUT
spins the hits
get on up
and strut
your stuff.
Just lick your lips
to the rhythm
of the yum-yum
TOP TEN MUSICAL DOUGHNUTS

Funky Nut-Ring
Punky Topping
Cinnamon Swing
Jazzy Jam-Jam
Raspberry Rap
Blueberry Bop
Honey Drip Hop
Sugar Mammy Pop
Spice Daddy Blues
Chocolate Boogaloo

So here's DJ DOUGHNUT
reminding you
that the hole's the thing
that makes a doughnut swing.

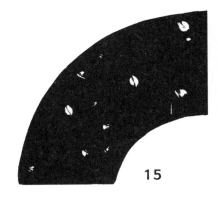

The Circle and the Square

Said the circle
to the square:
it appears
your corners
are all the same.
I've counted four
and bet you can't roll
as I can do
when I'm a ball.

Said the square
to the circle:
Good luck to you,
but isn't it the truth
that a ball must bear
the kicks of a boot?
So you roll where you go,
I'll stay right here
and be a window.

Said the circle
to the square:
O what a pity
you can't come with me
when I rise to the air
as a nice bright bubble.
And wait till you see
the full-moon I can be,
the best of round and yellow.

Said the square
to the circle:
Bubbles burst, as you know,
and many a night,
the moon doesn't show.
I'm happy, thank you,
to be a window.
I enjoy the view.
I am my own little sky.
I am the house's eye.

Mrs Harding on her Penny Farthing

Here comes Mrs Harding
on her Penny Farthing.
With head held high
and dress pulled low
she rides those two coins
wherever she goes.

People find it alarming
when she braves uphill
and dares downhill.
But she's never had a spill.
"Fear not," says Mrs Harding,
"I find it charming
to saddle these two coins.
Besides, didn't you know,
I'm the wind's darling."

Cloud Tricks

Wings wings.
The sky all wings.

But I
see no bird
see no kite
see no plane

Only clouds
playing
tricks again.

Globe

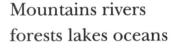

Spins like a ball
Round like a ball

In your hand it turns
And a whole world turns

Mountains rivers
forests lakes oceans

all one great swirl
of maps in motion

Spin it and spin it
till all countries orbit

in a merry-go-round
and everywhere gets a turn

to be upside down.

Zig-Zag Champion

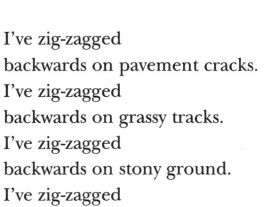

I don't need to brag
but I'm the zig-zag champion.
I won the Zig-Zag
Walking Backwards Marathon.

I've zig-zagged
backwards on pavement cracks.
I've zig-zagged
backwards on grassy tracks.
I've zig-zagged
backwards on stony ground.
I've zig-zagged
backwards through ups and downs.

And if you look at the shelf
you can see for yourself
the zig-zag trophy
of a zig-zag champion.

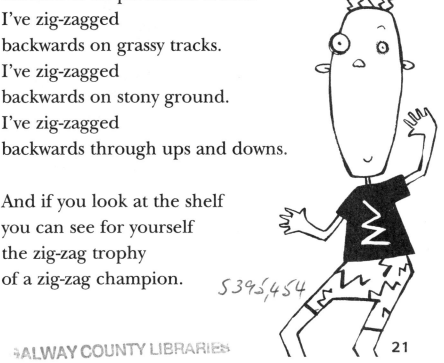

5395,454

A Friend for a Hot Day

I kindle fire
with my breath
I stir the flame
I raise the wind
Haven't you guessed yet?

I've been compared
to a peacock's tail
and I begin
with the sixth letter
of the alphabet.

My name is Fan.
Made in Japan.
Take me
in your
hand.

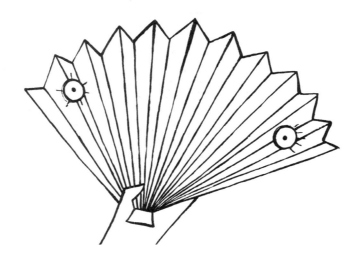

Halloween Pumpkin

Turn the lights down low
let the pumpkin glow
with triangle eyes
and triangle teeth
and a candle flame
for flickering brain
time to go trick or treat.

One Look at a Fishing Hook

What's an upside down
    question mark
    doing dangling
    in the dark
    of our river?

asked the little fish.

But the fisherman
who sat angling
had no answer.

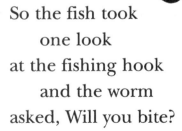

So the fish took
    one look
at the fishing hook
    and the worm
asked, Will you bite?

And the fish said, I

just might

but not tonight.

25

Sun and Moon on a Plate

How would you like your eggs?
Sunny side up
or moony side down?
said the waiter
to the clown.

Said the clown
to the waiter,
Young man, that depends
where the eggs are from –
chicken or alligator.

On second thoughts,
said the clown
with a wink,
I'll have a simple bowl
of cornflakes, I think.
But make sure you lay
the bowl sunny side up.

Sir, you always make my day,
said the waiter
to the clown.
And the waiter laughed and laughed
till both his eyes rolled
moony side down.

Follow that ⟶

A triangle with a tail.
I shot one into the air.
It fell to earth. Who knows where?
What good is one without a bow?
It points you where you wish to go.
My riddle's answer is arrow.

Shells

What do
horn shells
moon shells
tulip shells
turban shells
have in common?

Spirals said he
The sea said she

No No
It's the wind
it's the wind
said an echo

of eternity.

Hands Up
Who Knows the Answer

What has no hands
yet curves a yellow finger?

Banana.

What has no hands
yet points the right direction?

Compass.

What has no hands
yet stands with hands akimbo?

Teapot.

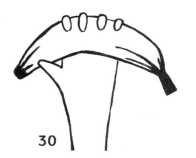

What has no hands
yet holds hands in a grip?

                   Handcuffs.

Perhaps.
Perhaps not.

                A wristwatch.

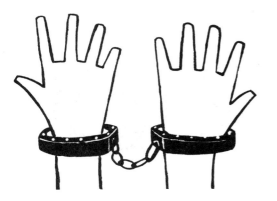

Making Wheels

The sun
makes a wheel
with spokes of light.

The spider
makes a wheel
with spokes of thread.

And I
make cartwheels
with spokes of my
arms and legs.

Under the Arch

Under the arch
of a bridge –
Who tells the river flow on?

Under the arch
of its back –
Why does the cat purr a song?

Under the arch
of a rainbow –
How do you find a pot of gold?

Under the arch
of night flowers –
What makes a little gnome so bold?

Under the arch
of an eyebrow –
Why do eyes twinkle with questions?

Inside of Me

I can't believe that jelly
cauliflower is my brain.

I can't believe that wriggly
sausage is my intestine.

I can't believe those gooey
red beans are my kidneys.

But they are mine, all mine.
Body parts that belong to me.

Yes, that throbbly pear
is actually my heart.

And my lungs, just there.
Why do they make me think of ham?

Please, no more diagrams
I'd rather not see

more of what's inside me.

35

Friends on a Shelf

Books are friends
that come
in squares
in rectangles
in oblongs

They have no eyes
yet stare
from across a shelf.
They ask no questions
yet contain
a world of whys.
They have no ears
yet listen
when things go wrong.

Books are friends
that come
in squares

in rectangles
in oblongs

And even when I break
my promise to read them,
they will be there, waiting,
the moment I need them.

R   A   I   N

R	A	I	N
a	w	n	o
t	a		
a	y	p	t
t		u	u
a	w	d	r
p	i	d	n
t	t	l	i
a	h	e	n
p		s	g
	s		
	u	w	b
	n	e	a
			c
		r	k
		u	
		n	

D R O P S

D	R	O	P	S
o	a	v	l	o
w	t	e	a	u
n	a	r	y	n
	t		i	d
w	a	f	n	s
e	p	i	g	
	t	e		l
c	a	l	r	i
o	p	d	a	k
m		s	t	e
e			a	
		a	t	f
		n	a	u
		d	p	n
			t	
		t	a	
		o	p	
		w		
		n		

39

The Hands of Trees

The hands of trees
reaching for air.
The hands of trees
clasped in a prayer.

The hands of trees
say welcome birds.
The hands of trees –
no need for words.

Lollipop

Who holds
a moon
that walks
on stilts?

Who holds
a ball
that stands
on a stick?

Who stops
all traffic
with a wave
of a lollipop wand?

Lollipop Lady.
Lollipop Man.

Cone I Spy

I know a cone
that sits on the road
watching wheels
go by
and it's a traffic
cone I spy.

I know a cone
that brings to my lips
a strawberry
smile
and it's an ice-cream
cone I spy.

I know a cone
that falls with a seed
from a tree
standing high

and it's a pine
cone I spy.

One sits on the road among traffic and smoke.
One has no choice but to melt down my throat.
One could be a jewel on a Christmas tree,
but I keep it in the pocket of my coat
where the eyes of the world can never see.

Mummy's Bump

Under her heart's thump-thump
sits Mummy's bump
a great huggy bump

and curled all cosy inside
could be my baby sister
could be my baby brother

having a water-ride
in the water-world
of Mummy's bump

having a turn to swing
from a wrinkly trapeze
of a navel string

and when I put my ears
to Mummy's bump
I hear the song of all the seas

and I hear myself begin.

(For Juliet, Dale and Omri)

Beach

Pebbles pebbles on the sand.
Grey eggs grey eggs in my hand.

This Boomerang Will Keep its Word

You threw me from Down Under
all the way to Over Yonder

Suddenly wood grew wings
and I was flying with the wind

Once I was part of a tree
you brought out the bird in me

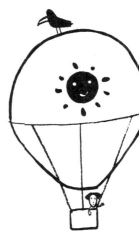

To your hand I will return
as bird to wood and wood to bird

This boomerang will keep its word
if you promise me one thing

Throw me once more to the wind
O throw me once more to the wind

Pick up a Poem
with another Orchard poetry book!

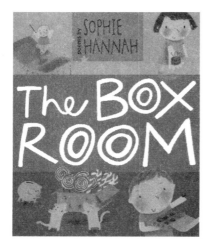

Zoo of Dreams
poems by Adrian Mitchell
pictures by Peter Bailey
ISBN 1 84121 817 0

**Fluff
and other stuff**
poems by Tony Mitton
pictures by Philip Hopman
ISBN 1 84121 813 8

The Box Room
poems by Sophie Hannah
pictures by Helen Stephens
ISBN 1 84121 793 X